making virtue reality
[actions] + contemplations

WRITTEN BY RUTH THOMPSON AND DESIGNED BY MARCIA GRACE

VirtueReality®

ETERNITY INK

MAKING VIRTUE REALITY
Copyright © 1997
Brahma Kumaris Raja Yoga Centres (Australia)
Published by Eternity Ink
78 Alt Street, Ashfield, NSW 2131 Australia
Tel: (02) 9990 7333 Fax: (02) 9799 3490
Email: indra@one.net.au
First Edition October 1998

Thompson, Ruth, 1961-
Making virtue reality: actions + contemplations.

ISBN 0 9587230 3 6.

1. Virtues – Meditations. I. Grace, Marcia, 1958- .
II. Prajapita Brahma Kumaris Ishwariya Vishwa
Vidyalaya (Abu, India). III. Title.

179.9

This book has been produced by Eternity Ink for
The Brahma Kumaris World Spiritual University, a
non-profit organisation, with the aim to share spiritual knowledge as a community service for the personal growth of individuals. The Brahma Kumaris
exists to serve the family of humanity: to assist individuals to discover and experience their own spiritu-
ality and personal growth; to understand the significance and consequences of individual action and
global interactions; and to reconnect and strengthen
their eternal relationship with the Supreme Soul, the
spiritual parent.

virtue reality

"We are at the centre of the circle, and there we sit while YES and NO chase each other around the circumference."

Chuang-tzu, the Taoist philosopher, has captured in a sentence the magic of a focussed mind. Most of us made daily use of this natural ability when we were children, constantly wondering, marvelling and working out the mystery of new objects and happenings. And now? How many times a day do Yes, No, and myriad other concerns intrude on our inner circle?

To keep focussed, to free ourselves from automatic thinking, we need to practise being reflective. The starting point, the first great mystery, is: "Who am I?" We turn our consciousness inwards, away from the concrete world of stereotypes and constant change. Inside we find our true selves: pure, changeless beings, characterised by universally celebrated qualities. By concentrating on ideas that nourish the soul we assimilate them into everyday awareness. Scattered, busy, emotive thinking gives way to deep, clear, original thinking. There is space for a true experience of peace and inner silence. Vitality fills the mind, and our outer world becomes a richer, more interesting place to be.

Our five senses constantly inform us of the world around us. What happens when we see something from a different angle? When touch and hearing are somehow paradoxical? When smell and taste provide new sensations? The mould is broken. We become enlivened. Our inner senses too, when exposed to fresh ideas, easily perceive new and exciting possibilities.

Open this book when you want to take off from old, familiar patterns. Reflect on the words and images. Try out the action ideas. Bring your thoughts, again and again, back to your chosen theme. Gradually delight, insight and certainty will flood the senses. Consciousness, our most precious and unique faculty, begins shining with this child's play of self-discovery.

[Today I will plan
to do something
I've never done
before.]

adventure

The wonder of being alive fills my being; there is
no space for fear or reliance on old comforts.
I gladly seek my part in the great drama of life.
Mountains and valleys lie before me:
sometimes disguised as a game, a job, a hobby,
a relationship. Sometimes delicate, sometimes
raw, sometimes mellow or compelling.
Exploring fresh perspectives, I willingly challenge
old ideas and images.
I feel timeless and invincible.

appreciative

I applaud generous actions, pure intentions
and unfolding talent. Simple things – like the
sound of rain, the industry of an office, the smell
of good food, the cry of a child – all offer
themselves to be valued and acclaimed.
I thank nature for reminding me of how order and
chaos each have their own time. I revel in
the worth, hidden or visible, that dwells in
each day of my life.

beauty

I find loveliness in myself and others, an
inner beauty, unique and cherished.
Twinkling behind wrinkled eyelids, or
shining through a newborn's face, an eternal grace
reveals itself. Even the bright, bare bones
of a winter tree show their own stark
tranquillity. I see the beauty that is, rather than
the beauty that could be: in the old and the new,
in the remarkable, the secret,
the rare and the common.

calm

In tune with my inner rhythm, I draw wisdom
from the past, allowing the future to shape
itself around me. My mind is a sanctuary
where shafts of golden sunlight laze as though
resting in the aisles of some great cathedral.
Everything is as it should be. I remain simple in
the midst of complexity, sure at times of unease,
and clear in the company of others.

centred

Like a finely balanced wheel aligned to its hub,
I am poised at the centre of myself,
of my world. My thoughts and feelings radiate
from the axis of 'self'. I am anchored to what is
real. Secure in myself and open-hearted, I see
other points of view without losing my own
identity. My connections with others are filled
with respect. I listen to my inner voice and watch
my actions flow from a point of peace.

Today I will enjoy
the fact that we
are all different.

cheerful

I catch the lightness of life and share it
with others. A childlike optimism floods my
senses, making difficulties seem like games to test
my talents. Bubbling away in my mind, like a
good, steady stream, is a whole-hearted concern
for the well-being of others. It spurs me
to see possibilities with clarity and confidence.
I sense a good future.

compassionate

I care for the honour of all beings, as a brother
to a brother, as a benefactor to a cause.
The patterns of humanity are full of mystery,
yet I have the heart to stay tuned to that
vast kaleidoscope of experience. I am part of it,
sharing all the sweet and bitter lessons of the
world. Realising the importance of each
human being, each creature, each plant, I learn
to be selfless in my love.

[Today I will be
on time.]

constant

Moving with life, not against it, I am naturally
steady. My inner journey is mirrored by
the passing seasons, by times of stillness and
times of sharing. There is fruitfulness in
the passage of time. Resolute, dependable, real,
I am never deceived by temporary gain.
Amidst fluctuations of fortune and health my
mind settles into the journey: continuous,
self-fulfilling, renewing.

> Today I will make
> a list of ten good
> things in my life.

content

I enjoy what life offers. Understanding its
ebb and flow, I know that my needs will be filled
as surely as the tide flows in. I wander the
shores of my experience, savouring the remarkable
variety. Sometimes seemingly worthless treasures
are tossed up to be re-examined. I care for each
one, worthy or worn-out, pleased with
the way my awareness is inspired. These inner
riches guide my soul into relationships of
giving and self-acceptance.

co-operative

I am generous with my time, always finding ways
to mould my talents for positive outcomes.
Willing to help and be helped, I bring tact and
adaptability into my relationships. Limitations do
not deter me. Heat and cold, light and dark
are helpers in the gardener's quest for
healthy growth. So, sensing the right time,
I help to harmonise the diverse energies that buzz
for attention until a job is done.

[Today I will get
on with a job I
have to do.]

courageous

Having glimpsed the truth, I hold on to it, undaunted by what I must do. Necessity makes me fearless. Risks challenge and deepen my maturity. I come straight from the heart, daring to be who I really am in the thousand challenges from birth to death. The rollercoaster of life thrills me and fills me with spontaneity and the urge to follow my passion.

[Today I will ask
new questions and
get new answers.]

creative

Imagining new ways to build on the past
transforms my present and inspires my future.
I empty my mind of the ordinary,
sensing the unformed creation and coaxing
its passage to light. The sweetness of this
struggle to distinctiveness is worth all my
commitment and love. Persevering, pioneering,
I am an adventurer of each new day.

detached

Loving without clinging, involved but not
dependent, I keep things in perspective.
I am who I am, free from others' design. I revere
the symphony of personalities that surround me.
They reveal the riches of life, unimpeded
by my own desires. Like the sun, lighting turn by
turn each land it crosses, I remain unbiased
and far-sighted, open to new prospects,
new notions.

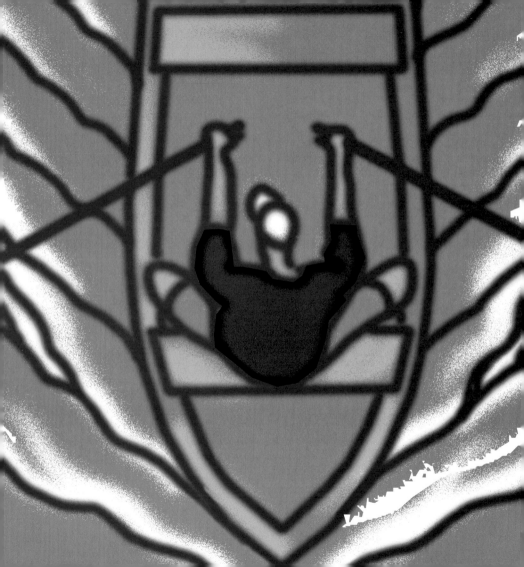

determined

Single-minded but flexible, like a river forging
its eternal route, I am dedicated to completions
and natural conclusions. There is nothing that
cannot be achieved. There is nothing that remains
permanent. I keep on moving with love and
purpose towards my destination.
My resolve is firm, my aims are clear.

dignified

I am serene in the midst of change, gracious and
confident with people. I stay at ease in
my environment, like a tree sending deep roots
into the earth to nourish its shade-giving
branches. I harmonise with change, knowing it as
a means of freedom and growth. There is purpose
in the course of time and events, and
I gladly work with that purpose. I choose to see
the best in myself and others so that I can
respond to virtue with virtue.

enthusiastic

A builder of dreams and ideas, I infuse life into
projects and tasks. Even the biggest
obstacles don't scare me. I relish the way they
draw on my powers to discern and accomplish.
Vigorous and keen, I encourage others
by affirming their special qualities. I inspire
myself by keeping sight of the opportunities
latent in every situation.

faithful

Loyal and true to my word, I am steadfast in
seeing things through. There is great solidity at
the core of my being for I am dedicated to
self-transformation. With unswerving confidence
in my purpose I challenge doubts and difficulties.
I look for broader perspectives and see the
interconnectedness of life and love.
Recognising God's love, I make a silent promise
to leave the world a better place.

Today I will be
open to new ideas
and suggestions.

flexible

I am carefree yet mindful; joyful yet calm;
strong and supple as bamboo.
I respond easily, and still hold my ground.
I can bend before the storm, bow gently in the
breeze, and reach for the sun when the air is just
a whisper. Resilience is part of my substance,
the very expression of my joy.

forgiving

I can see beyond immediate circumstances.
Clearing the decks of old grievances, I free myself
from outdated thinking. I learn from past
experiences and move on by tapping my inner
source of self-worth and humility.
Valuing honesty and commitment, I softly let go
and enable others to change. There are new
horizons, new growth, a new lease of life.

free

free

My soul is as free as a song whose every note
climbs a staircase of melody and light,
as if released in joy. No mind-set binds me.
No walls can darken my hope. My thoughts are
my own. I am committed to dissolving barriers
and honouring choices. I connect with God
as an angel would: inwardly supported,
stepping beyond limits.

generous

I am overflowing, unselfishly contributing,
a conduit for God's energy. There is great pleasure
in sharing what I have – a smile, a gift, a meal,
a story! I give freely of my heart, time and
attention. I give out of true benevolence, rather
than the need to be loved. What I give out flows
back, and so I my life is abundant.

gentle

I tread lightly upon this earth, seeing,
understanding, but never imposing.
Thoughtful, independent, I am gracious in victory
and defeat. I am free of possessiveness, so ease
of mind sweetens my relationships. My allegiance
to humanitarian ways heartens and inspires
others. Like the scent of a rose my untroubled
spirit imparts a lasting fragrance.

happy

The joy of being alive and in good company
flows through my being. Coursing through my
veins is the spirit of good fortune and high hopes.
A single glad thought changes my whole day.
Mine is the delight of shared experiences,
spontaneous and joyful. My interactions are full
of vibrancy. I live wholeheartedly.

healing

I gently return to equilibrium, nurtured by a
well-spring of love. My soul is washed and
soothed by the quiet energies of stillness.
Embracing the vastness of my inner landscape,
I understand the cycles of growth and decay.
They lead me back to my original wholeness.
Each part of my soul, blemished or sound, offers
a key to completion. I explore what
is proffered with an open heart, and connect
with the source of purity.

Today I will clean
out my drawers
and cupboards.

honest

I am truthful in thought, forthright in speech
and trustworthy in actions. I care about the
qualities I contribute to relationships. This is the
way I honour friends and colleagues.
My motives are clean, so my thoughts and
feelings can dance in the daylight.
Being open with others challenges me to
be my natural self.

humility

I value others without seeking their attention.
Self-respect is my inner light;
I need nothing extra. I am unafraid of life's great
teachings, in all their daily guises.
As the giant tree bows in the storm,
so I salute truth. Transformation is the mode of
travel on my spiritual path.

sense of humour

Surprising events and unusual outcomes delight
my spirit and illuminate the day.
Sometimes impulsive, like a child compelled by
the sheer pleasure of play, I enjoy sharing laughter
with others. I have an eye for hidden virtue
and unexpected value, a love for paradox, for light
and shadow. I am ready to see the often
unusual conjunctions of truth and falsehood.

Today I will visit
the library and
allow a book to
find me.

intuitive

I perceive the inner rhythm of events, and allow
my feelings to guide me. The core of things,
that which is intrinsic to a personality or situation,
naturally attracts me. I trust the subtle cues of
my inner voice, unclouded by ordinary thoughts
and intentions. My convictions are fuelled
by the wisdom of foresight. I understand the
implications of things which I initiate.

integrity

My actions reflect what I value most – I am the
same inside and out. I aim to work with the
highest values. My head and heart are connected
when I adhere to the laws of humanity,
the principles of love and truth. There is a sense
of wholeness as I work within the intricate web of
our human family.
I salute the aspirations of those around me.

loving

My love is a gift, free from anticipation.
In the safe harbour of my soul there are no special
conditions. The deepest current of
my being is a selfless desire for others' happiness.
I infuse this warmth into everything I do.
With a big heart I can naturally love myself and
others, with all our idiosyncrasies. I listen
with my heart, to the heart, letting everyone
know of the loveliness I see.

Today I will
examine my dreams
for answers and
reminders.

magical

I live in the moment, able to catch its significance
before it passes. Reality is fluid with possibility.
There is wonder in the tiniest particle.
Simply by believing in possibilities,
I turn loss into benefit, the ordinary into
extraordinary. Such a marvellous gift
is free for the asking. Like the miracle of flowers
after a long winter, it emerges whenever
I invite imagination.

nurturing

Constantly supportive and available, I open up
pathways by guiding with love and
inventiveness. I nourish and encourage, like a
parent teaching a child to walk, like an
artist cradling an idea until it thrives, like a nurse
fostering a patient to health. Listening, seeing,
contributing, in often unseen ways, I provide the
warmth of tenderness and experience.

[Today I will stop
rushing around
and check to see
what's driving me.]

patient

I allow the fruits of my actions to ripen in their own time. I am a gardener of life's phases, not hungry for early results. Whenever there are storms, I prepare, work carefully, and let events unfold at their own pace. Happy occasions inspire me to savour each moment without rushing on to the next. Knowing when it is right to wait, I gently allow the future to emerge.

peaceful

With great calm I observe the flow of my mind,
then welcome inner silence. There is harmony
in my thoughts and feelings, and a sense of
generous detachment. My mind is mirror-like: a
tranquil lake clearly reflecting the busy movement
of everyday life. Inner work continues
at the deepest levels, helping me to stay
calm and bright.
I bask in the coolness of this power.

positive

The seed of my thoughts and actions is hope:
good wishes for every soul and all of nature.
My optimism generates an atmosphere of
certainty that whatever happens is for the best.
Reality will eventually echo my vision and reflect
my sincerity. I have a lot of energy for creating,
for getting on with things. Even if I get
sidetracked I know how to take stock and drive
with confidence in the right direction.

practical

Clear-headed, I thrive on getting things done.
I am never hijacked by impossible goals and am
always willing to search for solutions.
Down to earth and realistic, I enjoy finding the
facts and making things work.
I am a veteran of overcoming difficulties,
skilled in the arts of adjusting and setting
priorities. I sort through the visions for wings
that will make each new task fly.

pure-hearted

I love and converse with the pristine part of my
soul, and connect with the purity in others.
I kindle the light of self-respect. Discovering my
innocence of spirit teaches me to realise the
virtues in those around me. I see every soul as a
diamond, each facet revealing a different strength
or quality. Even when the diamond is encrusted
by harsh memories, I look for the sparkle that
tells me of the real personality.

resourceful

I uncover ways to release hidden potential, giving
heart to others that the key can always be found.
Even if I have to dig down to the bottom,
I know my bag of solutions will never be empty.
Answers to dilemmas and predicaments
always turn up, like clues to riddles with
wonderfully simple explanations. Inventive and
imaginative, I glide through life as
gently as a breeze.

respectful

Valuing the unique role of each person,
I acknowledge even the smallest contribution.
I am considerate of the needs of others, and leave
room for people to be their true selves.
When unfathomable events or people cross my
path, I appreciate their mystery without making
hasty judgements. I honour the cycles within
our lives by filling unions and partings with
the light of unqualified trust.

responsible

I fulfil my commitments and guarantee
my co-operation. The grand theatre of life
teaches me to balance spontaneity with reliability,
easiness with vigilance. I care for outcomes
and how they affect people. I take care of my
own well-being, knowing that others
will gain from my healthy attitudes and
broad perspectives.

self-confident

I am in touch with my dreams and willing to work
with reality. Self-reliant, I love to instigate ideas
and projects that tap my individuality and nurture
my relationships. Vigour and candour are
characteristics I respond to with ease.
Keeping in mind that tests will come to
strengthen my resolve, I trust my destiny.
I know my powers and limitations, and choose
my goals clearly and assuredly.

strong

Throughout the seasons of fruitfulness and decay
the mountain remains, supporting each season in
its own time. So I support myself and others with
initiative and commitment of spirit.
When obstacles and opposition come I find
the deep, quiet place inside me that responds with
positivity and decisiveness.
My resolution is toughened, my vision is purified.
My strength is who I am.

Today I will phone or write to an old friend to say hello.

sweet

The selfless care of a grandparent, the innocent ways of a child sharing, the sudden thoughtfulness of a friend, or unexpected help from colleagues all recall the heartfelt exclamation "How sweet of you!" So I strive to make my presence like fresh air: a welcome flow of soothing, positive energy. Knowing there is good in everything, I see beyond the shadows. Mine is the pleasure of being able to give.

tolerant

I have the maturity to let go of expectations, and
the love to keep on giving. Much more than
withstanding adversity, I harness the depth of my
resources. My powers of endurance and renewal
accompany me into the trickiest situations, like a
favourite coat that I take wherever I go.
I always bounce back, complying with change,
prospering from the game.

trusting

Knowing that the ups and downs of life
are opportunities in disguise, I accept the
journey at hand. Sometimes, looking
into the future is like trying to see into the depth
of a fast flowing river. Instead of struggling
against the current, I swim faster, with it. Events
carry me, filling the gaps of my experience,
fulfilling my purpose of becoming whole.
I thank the people who help me to realise and
define my strength.

truthful

I am straightforward and unbiased in all my
dealings, unafraid of speaking about what is in my
heart. When conflicting feelings weigh me down
I make time to clarify them, so that what
I communicate is genuine and responsive. Seeing
things for what they are, myself included,
I manifest the potential that God sees in me.
I love the secrets of the universe as they reveal
themselves in my life.

uncomplicated

Seeing to the heart of the matter, I stay with
what's real and keep my life simple.
I allow my natural, childlike wisdom to guide me
to the easiest path. It makes me a natural learner.
I can laugh about my mistakes, thank them for
making things clear, and move on.
Every day I gratefully let something go, making
space in my life for new ideas and experiences.
Every day I remember my own essence.

> Today I will
> balance time for
> myself and time
> for others.

wise

Nothing can surprise me. I understand that complexity has its roots in simplicity, that everything has a beginning, middle and end. Endings are preludes to beginnings, and so I don't make assumptions about what should happen next. I act, only after observing, listening and accepting. Having done my work, I step back and let things take their course.

about meditation

*Taking a few minutes every day, I turn within
to my place of creative solitude...*

I explore the small and great questions of life, gradually rejoicing
in who and what I am. In moments of reverie it is easy to feel
close to the source of virtue, it is easy to be connected with the
One. I absorb the calming flow of peace and power, and my
spirits soar like a bird gliding on a slipstream.

My mind is naturally poised in the light of God. I can feel the
benevolent mind of God, like a whisper of love stirring my soul.
Subtle treasures infuse my senses.

They are part of me, part of my purpose of being. Radiating
clear, bright thoughts I return refreshed.

Picture Credits

ACORN PHOTOAGENCY: **6, 52** – Laurie Taylor;
38, 68, 84, 90 – R. Frith; **36, 88** – Dolly Van Zaane;
46 – Ron Sacerdoti; **76** – Brent Sumner;
92 – Steve Perkins

AUSTRAL INTERNATIONAL: **4,14, 18, 22, 74, 78**

BRAHMA KUMARIS: **54**

DEBORAH BRILL: **20, 24, 60, 82**

IMAGE BANK: **26** – *Dynamism of a Dog on a Leash*
Giaccomo Balla 1912, oil on canvas, Albright-Knox Art
Gallery Buffalo, New York. Bequest of A. Conger
Goodyear and Gift of George F. Goodyear, 1964;
32 – *Child Enthroned* Thomas Cooper Gotch, Bridgeman Art
Library; **86** – *A Mountain Stream in Snow,* a Hiroshige print

KEEP AUSTRALIA BEAUTIFUL COUNCIL: **50**

MARCIA GRACE: **10, 30, 44, 96, 100**

NELL SMITH: **12, 48, 62, 72, 80, 94**

PHOTODISC: **16, 28, 34, 40, 42, 56, 58, 66, 98**

SEAN O'SHEA: **8, 64**

RUDOLPH ZWAMBORN: **70**

Acknowledgements

For all their kind contributions – Robert Frith, Karen
Phillips, Michael Blythe, Alan Anstey, Peter Robertson,
Keep Australia Beautiful Council, Helen Northey, Sean
O'Shea, Jaie Watts, Carmen Warrington, Rodolph

RUTH THOMPSON, AUTHOR

As a University Project Officer, I find more than enough workplace quandaries to deepen my virtue practice! Practising and teaching Raja Yoga Meditation for more than 15 years has been pivotal to gaining ground (and making up lost ground) in this sometimes slippery terrain. Warm thanks go to the many souls who, often inadvertently, helped kindle and stoke the creative fires. This book celebrates the one project that has no deadlines.

MARCIA GRACE, DESIGNER

I am a graphic designer and meditator of more than 10 years. Through the inception, development and production of this book, I have had the happiness of experiencing many virtues of those who have helped so easily and naturally in its creation.

ETERNITY INK is publisher for the Brahma Kumaris World Spiritual University. If you wish to find out about the free meditation courses offered by the Brahma Kumaris World Spiritual University, contact the main centre closest to you:

WORLD HEADQUARTERS:	PO BOX No 2, Mount Abu, Rajasthan, 307501, India
	Tel: (2974) 2248
AUSTRALIA:	78 Alt St, Ashfield NSW 2131 Tel (02) 9716 7066
BRAZIL:	R. Dona Germaine Burchard, 589 - Sao Paulo
	SP 05002-062 Tel (11) 864 3694
HONG KONG:	17 Dragon Rd, Causeway Bay, Tel (5) 806 3008
INDIA:	25 New Rohtak Rd, Karol Bagh, New Delhi 110005
	Tel (11) 752 8516
KENYA:	PO Box 12349, Maua Close, off Parklands Road Westlands
	Nairobi Tel (2) 743 572
SINGAPORE:	287 Holland Road Tel: (65) 467 1742
MALAYSIA:	10 Lorong Maarof, Bangsar Park 59000 Kuala Lumpur
	Tel: (03) 282 2310
NEW ZEALAND:	51 Rockfield Road, One Tree Hill, Auckland
	Tel: (09) 579 5646
PHILIPPINES:	7484 Bagtikan Cnr, Dao Sts, San Antonio Village, Makati
	Metro-Manila Tel: (02) 890 7960
THAILAND:	85/156-7 MU 4, Chaeng Wattana Road, Pakkret, Nonthaburi
	Bangkok Tel: (02) 573 8242
UK:	65 Pound Lane, London NW10 2HH, UK Tel (181) 459 1400
RUSSIA	35, Prospecct Andropova, Moscow 15487 Tel (95) 112 51 2
USA:	Global Harmony House, 46 South Middle Neck Rd, NY
	11021 Tel (516) 773 0971